THE INTERNATIONAL SATANIC NETWORK EXPOSED

Survivors Reveal Names of Presidents, Prime Ministers and Royals

ISBN 979-8-9878667-3-3 (print)

First edition: December 2023.

Visit the author's website at
www.TheFreedomArticles.com.

Table of Contents

"Pedophilia and Satanism are the cement that hold the establishment control structure together in every country."

– David Icke

"Humanity is actually under the control of dinosaur-like alien reptiles called the Babylon Brotherhood who must consume human blood to maintain their human appearance."

– David Icke

"The families in positions of great financial power obsessively interbreed with each other. But I'm not talking about one Earth race, Jewish or non-Jewish. I'm talking about a genetic network that operates through all races, this bloodline being a fusion of human and reptilian genes."

– David Icke

*****

Introduction

This book will probably shock, outrage and thoroughly disgust you. If so, you are having a natural, normal response to a scale of evil that exists on Earth which is beyond imagination for some people. Nonetheless, it is true, and we are concerned with what is true and real here, not fake. It is always better to know the truth, however dark and ugly, than to live in delusion and ignorance.

The information in this book is obviously difficult to verify in the traditional sense. The acts being committed here are clearly so criminal and demonic that it is not like we can easily get evidence in the forms of videos and pictures to prove all the evil deeds in black and white (although, this book does cover some of what we have), since obviously, the perpetrators of these acts are dedicated to keeping them secret. Having said that, the testimony of those strong and brave enough to have survived SRA (Satanic Ritual Abuse) is incredibly compelling – and all the more so when the separate, independent testimony of one person corroborates another person's. As you will see, this theme of overlapping testimony occurs throughout this book, lending strong credibility to the claims made by the survivors and witnesses.

A quick opening note: some may squabble over the exact definitions of Satanism and

Luciferianism, saying that they are not the exact same thing, and that Satanism is not necessarily 'evil' since the root word Satan simply means 'the opposer,' and that Satanism is opposed to puritanical religion and unjust authority.

The purpose of this book is to help expose an international network which uses black magic in their rituals and ceremonies, including things such as rape, torture, animal and human sacrifice, murder and cannibalism. For simplicity, I will be labelling this network as the international Satanic network, regardless of the debate over the exact definition of Satanism, or the version of Satanism put forward by organizations such as The Satanic Temple[1], which lists among

---

1 https://thesatanictemple.com/pages/about-us

its foundational tenets that "one should strive to act with compassion and empathy" and that "one's body is inviolable, subject to one's own will alone" because that is clearly not the form of Satanism we are exposing here in this book. Throughout the book, I will refer to the perpetrators of SRA and practitioners of Satanism as the NWO (New World Order) controllers, manipulators or criminals. I do this because the the people into this deep level of Satanism are the very same people hellbent on transforming the planet into a worldwide dictatorship they have dubbed the NWO – with themselves at the helm of course.

The evidence that follows shows that the international Satanic network is a vast interlocking system that is structured and operated very much like a giant multinational corporation, with various divisions, branches and regional directors. This book arranges the testimonies – all of which appear to be credible and valid – so that the most detailed information will be towards the end, especially in chapters 11 to 15. It is always good to think critically and have a skeptical mind, but to those with a closed mind, be warned: this information will shock and overwhelm you.

Finally, please note that there is no way to discuss Satanism without also discussing the New World Order, and also no way to discuss it without also discussing the extraterrestrial issue. As you will discover throughout this book, but especially in chapter 14 with the testimony of Arizona Wilder, extraterrestrial or interdimensional Reptilians are totally intertwined with Satanism; there is no way to fully talk about Satanism without mentioning the Reptilians. In many cases, and perhaps in all cases, they are the ones conducting the rituals to achieve a certain benefit. Again, it may sound hard to believe and 'out there' however please take a look at the evidence first before discounting the concept out of hand.

This book is only written to be a brief summary of Satanism and the international Satanic network, providing a window into a very real and dark world from which our ordinary world is controlled. There is a plethora of further evidence about it, and you, dear reader, are encouraged to do your own research to confirm the information presented here and go beyond it.

Chapter 1 – The Cremation of Care Ceremony at Bohemian Grove

Before we get into the all the survivor testimonies, it's worth revisiting an exceptional piece of undercover journalism performed by the infamous Alex Jones, founder of Infowars.com, who managed not only to sneak into Bohemian Grove on July 15th 2000, but actually managed to record one of the black magic rituals there. The footage (still online in various places such as here[2]) is not the best quality but it's good enough to get an idea of what is going on.

In this dark ceremony, robed and hooded figures stand at the base of a 40 foot owl. They then 'sacrifice' (although it appears to be a mock sacrifice) a victim they call "Care," presumably as an offering to owl deity who represents an old biblical god Molech (also spelt Moloch) who was known to eat children. This is why the entire ritual is called "The Cremation of Care" since it enacts the

---

2 https://odysee.com/@TheTruthWillSetYouFree:a/Bohemian-Grove-'00:a

murder, killing and burial of care, which is an extension of or equivalent to the emotion of compassion and love. To the right is a photo of a statue of Moloch or Molech at the Colosseum in Rome, Italy.

So what is the meaning of this ritual? The obvious interpretation is that its purpose is to shun, ignore, reduce, bury or completely eliminate the caring part of whomever participates in it. It encourages the watchers and participants to sacrifice the good part of themselves – their caring nature. Care represents heart-based intelligence, empathy and compassion. This brings to mind the testimony of elite banking whistleblower Ronald Bernard (see chapter 9), who used to rub shoulders with the people who really run the world (beyond the level of puppet politicians like presidents and prime ministers) – the people looking to set up the NWO worldwide totalitarian dictatorship. As Ronald got deeper and deeper into the game, and more and more comfortable with committing acts of evil, he was introduced to situations where these NWO criminals were sacrificing children. That was enough to make him sick to his stomach and get the hell out of there. Ronald specifically recalls that when he started working in that whole world, someone experienced in that industry told him that he would need to put his conscience in a freezer (i.e. on ice) to make it. Otherwise, he wouldn't go far. The point was that he was advised to kill his compassion or care in order to advance.

The Cremation of Care, and other dark rituals like it, are Satanic initiation ceremonies where demonic possession can occur. Though the various ritualistic elements (fire, music, costume, drama, darkness, etc.) the participant is put into an altered state of consciousness – in fact, a hypnotic state. This state can open a kind of portal where some form of lower or demonic consciousness can influence and overtake the participant. It's a 2-way street; the participant gets a rush of energy and feels like they are gaining superhuman powers, so they perceive they are getting something, while the demonic consciousness takes over part of their mind and/or soul. They become more of a slave to this consciousness. This phenomenon is summed up by the famous saying "he sold his soul to the devil." I will expand on this theme later in the book.

Chapter 2 – The Testimony of Jeanette Archer

Jeanette Archer was born into a multigenerational family cult of SRA in the UK. She somehow managed to survive, despite being frequently raped and tortured. She was sold into a pedophile ring as a girl so that her father could make money off her. In interviews like this[3], she describes how her grandfather was the head of the cult. He taught his children how to sexually abuse their children, how to conduct home rituals (e.g. drowning in the bathtub) and how to sacrifice babies whose blood was harvested for Satanic blood drinking. These are all common themes in Satanism: the perpetuation within a family over generations, the head of the cult teaching (or programming) the children and grandchildren to treat those weaker than them or dependent upon them cruelly and the encouraging of parents to sell their children into the cult to make money off them.

Rituals were done on the farm owned by Jeanette's grandfather, as well as in a

---

[3] https://web.archive.org/web/20200723074746/https://www.youtube.com/watch?v=IcLNFzXafCw

hospital morgue. She personally witnessed child sacrifice, on a concrete slab, performed by high-up cult members. Jeanette felt as though she would die all the time – she was even made to measure her own coffin.

This kind of activity is horrid and nauseating, however it is real and is still happening today. We must face the truth of this, without denial, as the first step to exposing and overcoming it.

Chapter 3 – The Testimony of Kristy Allen

Kristy Allen was born into an American military family; her dad, a CIA agent, peddled child pornography, sold her to the US Military and continually raped her sisters. All were used in sexual Satanic ritual carried out by the card-carrying members of the CIA and the Mormon Church. She experienced gang rape and witnessed Satanists killing children and eating out their hearts.

Kristy said the following in this presentation[4] before the ITNJ (International Tribunal for Natural Justice) Judicial Commission, highlighting how the use of abuse and torture to create dissociation and multiple personalities/alters is central to the way Satanists operate:

"Ritualistic child abuse is the most hideous of all abuse. The basic objective is to systematically terrorize children until they are forced to dissociate. The torture is the

---

4 https://www.youtube.com/watch?v=ixHC8lm82Qg

execution of a well-planned, well-thought out ritual often performed by close relatives. The only escape for the children is to dissociate, where they will develop a new personality to enable them to endure the abuse. This new personality is very helpful for the abusers. Once the abuse is over, the core personality is not conscious of what happened. Dissociation also serves the purpose of the occult, because the children have no day-to-day memories of the atrocities ... the victims lead relatively normal lives, until they get triggered, and flashbacks or nightmares occur."

According to Kristi, there is a mindset in the US Military where they believe that someone in their ranks has been given to them, and that they control and own them as well as their families (wife and children). It uses the verb "issue" to describe this, i.e. the children have been "issued" to the military for their use (i.e. to abuse and turn into sex slaves). Kristy knew others from military families who were sold into slavery; they were told that they could be famous musicians if they agreed to be a drug mule or to traffic weapons.

Kristi's sister was also caught up in the Satanic cult. At first she didn't believe her sister when she talked about SRA, but then after Kristy personally attended a public speech by Cathy O'Brien (see chapter 10), she spoke to Cathy afterwards, which helped confirm her memories were real. Kristi's sister was made into a 'breeder' which is another common theme among Satanism – the Satanists use some of their female sex slaves to literally breed children. They impregnate them, then later on kill the baby in Satanic ritual. Kristi names Bill Clinton as being involved as says he made her sister into a "call girl."

Chapter 4 – The Testimony of David Shurter

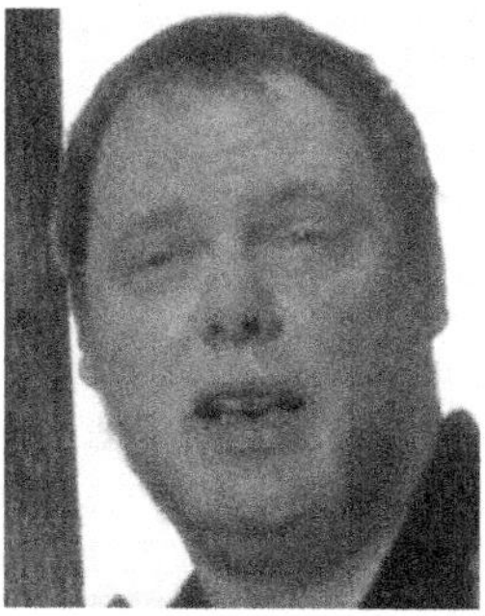

David Shurter is another SRA victim who was taken to Bohemian Grove as a child. He personally witnessed child sacrifice there, led by NSA agent and known Satanist Colonel Michael Aquino, whose name crops up again and again in this book. Shurter was also part of the infamous Omaha Nebraska child trafficking ring which was exposed by then senator John DeCamp in his 1992 book on the Franklin Cover-up (more on this in chapter 8).

In interviews such as these[5], David reveals how he was sexually abused by both his own parents and others in the Satanic cult into which he was thrown. It took him until he reached middle age to uncover the gruesome childhood memories of SRA and to fully grasp the significance of it. He says "I was never involved in an actual child abduction, but I was involved in the ritual murders of children."

---

5 https://www.youtube.com/watch?v=d9__tMLGZUc

The cult leaders anticipated that David would be involved in the cult for life, but he managed to break free, however he had to overcome the humiliation of speaking publicly about everything that had happened to him.

David highlights how the growing sexualization of children and worldwide push for pedophilia (trying to make the age of consent lower and lower) is a manifestation of Satanism. It represents the violation of innocence and theft of purity. Just because a child's body can be sexually aroused at 10 years old doesn't mean that that child is psychologically and emotionally mature enough to engage in sex; thus, sex between an adult and a child will necessarily always reflect a power imbalance, with the adult pedophile holding all the power. Many people and lawmakers all over the world have recognized this principle, which is why most countries have strict laws forbidding pedophilia.

According to David, the Cremation of Care ritual at Bohemian Grove is a mock sacrifice only, with 2,000 men attending. He also mentions that, after the Oprah interview with Michael Aquino[6], Oprah was contacted by 800 victims of Aquino and SRA.

---

[6] https://www.bitchute.com/video/9xYiN0CkoFGh/

In his book *Rabbit Hole: A Satanic Ritual Abuse Survivor's Story Paperback*[7], David exposes the dark underbelly of Satanism in Omaha, Nebraska, including cover-ups, kidnappings, child murders and pedophile rings. It's a sad but by now familiar story: the people in the highest positions of power in Omaha perpetrated unspeakable acts of abuse on children, including murdering them. Omaha was (and may still be) a microcosm of the larger international Satanic story which has spread its tentacles all over the world.

---

[7] https://www.amazon.com/Rabbit-Hole-Satanic-Ritual-Survivors/dp/0984893717

Chapter 5 – The Testimony of Jolene Seebacher

Jolene Seebacher is another former mind control and SRA victim, but with a twist: she was born with enhanced supernatural abilities and became a subject of black ops military programming. She somehow survived SRA when other victims around her were sacrificed. She exposes[8] how the Satanic calendar contains specific sacrificial dates – the Satanists privately use sciences such as astrology and sacred geometry to calculate the best dates for their rituals while using their front organizations to publicly denounce such things as pseudoscience.

She also reveals how the perpetrators use black magic to gain power, such as spell casting and blood sacrifice. She says she saw the Satanists put devices on their victims to measure the energy frequencies the victims were giving off. She recalls that she was repeatedly physically and sexually abused by a "circle of bald men" in Satanic ritual with sigils, chanting, candles and

[8] https://web.archive.org/web/20170105095331/https://www.youtube.com/watch?v=hJltG0iR-dc

buckets of blood. We know that Satanists derive pleasure from other's pain in sadistic style. Not only do they enjoy the theft of innocence from raping and killing children, but also, according to Jolene, they use the innocent energy of children to open up supernatural portals. She recalls experiences where this happened – where they opened up portals and then demonic and Egyptian beings walked through to this dimension.

On this note, Jolene has used her horrific experiences for good; she moved into the field of psychic self defense. She specializes in helping all types of targeted individuals (TIs).

Chapter 6 – The Testimony of Zachary King

Zachary King is another person with firsthand experience in the world of Satanism. He reveals how he was actually a former Satanic High Wizard. He got into this by joining a Satanic coven as a youth. In interviews such as this one[9], he discusses how he was a normal American boy in an average neighborhood who grew up in a Baptist home. He began practicing magic at age 10, joined a Satanic coven at 13 and had broken all ten biblical commandments by the time he was 15.

Initially, he just liked practicing magic. Once he realized it was real and actually worked to manifest things, he wanted to do it more. At the beginning he thought the coven was just about getting drunk, getting high and getting laid. It wasn't long before he was sexually molested and abused by older women in the cult, a pattern that would continue. As he got deeper into it, he was told that he would need to soak in the urine and blood of pigs, and sign his own name in blood, to be fully

---

[9] https://www.youtube.com/watch?v=Q0FJKdtOAm0

initiated. He describes how the coven was part of a child sex ring.

Things kept getting stranger and more evil. He was asked to participate in Satanic sexual initiatory rites. One of them included the intention to deliberately get a 15-year-old girl pregnant, then sacrifice her baby. This theme – of intentional abortions and human sacrifice – crops up again and again in the world of Satanism.

Zach went to Bohemian Grove for the first time in 1988. He says it is a men's only event with open homosexuality, where gay strippers and gay porn stars are hired. Zach reveals that in addition to the now infamous Cremation of Care ritual (as discussed in chapter 1), there is other black magic that happens at Bohemian Grove. There is public magic spell work that happens near the giant 40 foot owl, and there is private magic spell work that happens behind closed doors. He was asked to mediate between two people who didn't get along, as well as perform black magic spells where certain people were astrally targeted with harm. He says that High Wizards are approached and asked to cast spells on people to ensure they are made to cooperate or have an 'accident.'

He names names – including US Presidents – who he personally saw at Bohemian Grove. He says he saw Ronald Reagan, and that he looked highly uncomfortable. He also saw the Bushes (George Sr. and Jr.) and Bill

Clinton. Interestingly, he mentions he saw Hillary Clinton walk in to tell Bill something, even though it was a men's only event, and that she was quickly escorted by security.

Zach states that there is an organized Satanic world network. He was in his Satanic coven until about 18, then joined the World Church of Satan, a much bigger, worldwide cult, with its own CEO and Board of Directors. It was in this organization that he attained the position called High Wizard. His job was to travel around the world doing whatever spells people wanted him to do – rock stars, movie stars, politicians, the rich … he said there was no limit to who would want a spell and what they'd be willing to pay for it.

Chapter 7 – The Testimony of Kathy Collins

Former SRA and mind control victim Kathy Collins is another one who went through the horrors of torture and abuse. Fortunately, she came out the other side being able to forgive. In this interview[10] with Bill Ryan (co-founder of Project Camelot), she reveals how she pulled herself out of victimhood and healed her trauma. This is an inspirational story of SRA recovery which can serve as a guide for others.

Kathy was in MK Ultra – specifically the Project Monarch program, one of the 149 MK Ultra sub projects that took its name from the Monarch butterfly. The NWO manipulators use butterfly symbolism to represent the transformation of the person, not in a positive way (as most people would think, or as most people would associate with butterflies) but in a way that turns an innocent child into a victim who is controllable and under their spell. This often means a sex slave or an assassin. For them,

10 https://www.youtube.com/watch?v=_stICUMOWhc

the butterfly symbolizes becoming enslaved not empowered.

I discuss MK Ultra more in chapter 10, and I have already alluded to this theme in earlier chapters, but here it is again: through various techniques such as hypnosis, rape, torture and abuse, the mind of the victim is split into a honeycomb of personalities or 'alters,' each unaware of the others because of amnesic barriers. These alters are then programmed to be or do certain things without the others knowing. In this way, an undetectable spy, sex slave or assassin can be created.

In this chapter, I will focus more on the specifics of Project Monarch (information from this website[11]):

Much of Project Monarch remains classified. From the information that has leaked out, it is easy to see why these mind-control experiments were considered top secret. Project Monarch was officially begun by the U.S. Army in the early 1960s, and it is still classified as top secret for reasons of national security. Some researchers are quite certain that Monarch evolved from such MK-ULTRA subprojects as Spellbinder, established to

[11] https://web.archive.org/web/20230824124006/https://12bytes.org/articles/exposed/project-monarch-satanism-and-child-sexual-abuse/

create "Manchurian Candidate" assassins, and Operation Often, which explored black magic and the occult.

Researcher Ron Patton theorizes that the name Monarch had nothing to do with royalty, but referred to the Monarch butterfly and "the feeling of light-headedness," as if one were "floating or fluttering like a butterfly," after undergoing the trauma induced by electroshock. One may also think of the common occult symbolism of the butterfly for the soul or the mind and an ancient belief that human souls become butterflies while they are between lives awaiting reincarnation.

Patton states that Monarch was essentially about programming the mind, modifying human behavior, and placing its subjects into a "marionette syndrome." A marionette is a puppet whose actions are determined by a puppeteer pulling its strings, hence the analogy concerning the psychologist and the programmed subject. Conventional psychologists might use the term "conditioned stimulus response sequences," but the Monarch experimenters called the process "Imperial conditioning." Monarch also diverged greatly from traditional psychological conditioning exercises by including satanic rituals in order to enhance the trauma experienced by the subject. The programmer might choose to intensify the rituals by having the hypnotized or drugged subject "image" ancient archetypal symbols of mysticism and the occult, such as spiders, bats, snakes, masks, castles, mazes, demons, and monsters.

Monarch programming had six levels:

Alpha: General conditioning designed to improve memory retention, visual acuity, and physical strength. Exercises deliberately subdivided the subject's personality and emphasized the left-brain/right-brain division.

Beta: Sexual programming that would eliminate all moral values and remove all inhibitions.

Delta: Deadly force programming for special agents and elite forces of the military. Subjects were conditioned to have no fear, and subliminal instructions were implanted for the agent to commit suicide if captured.

Theta: Psychic programming through various electronic mind-control systems, brain implants, and telemetry devices. The implants were used with highly advanced computers and satellite tracking systems.

Omega: Also known as "Code Green," this level involved self-destruct programming that caused the subject/agent to commit suicide if too much memory was retrieved by interrogation.

Gamma: This level activated itself within a subject/agent when an opportunity arose wherein misinformation and deception could be disseminated to great advantage.

...

The methods are unspeakably brutal and sadistic. Monarch Programming begins early in a Monarch slave's life. They are taken "as infants and traumatized using electroshocks, drugs, sexual abuse, mind games, and hypnosis in order to force the mind to split and create an alternative personality to deal with the pain. The victim imagines that someone else is being tortured and the mind is forced to split. Each personality (or alter, as in 'alternate personality') is then programmed and trained to perform specific tasks and missions." The focus is to traumatize the victim to such a degree that their personality is destroyed or fractured and the person is then "reprogrammed" by their "programmer." They become a mind-controlled slave who can be triggered at anytime to perform any action required by their handler. The difference between a Handler and a Programmer is this: Programmers program monarch slaves and

Handlers monitor and oversee fully programmed slaves who have been entrusted in their "care".

Kathy was born in Santa Rosa, California, which is a big center for mind control. She was taken to the Presidio Child Development Center (in San Francisco) which was at one point was investigated by the FBI in 1987 due to the slew of allegations that it was a hub of child molestation. Those interested can read more about that here[12].

At a young age, she underwent sexual abuse (perpetrated by both men and women), was made into a child prostitute, and was experimented upon with drugs, electroshock and strobe lights. She recalls being carted away in a potato sack by her father. At age three, she remembers being taken through an initiation ritual and being forced to drink blood.

The Bohemian Grove, property of the Bohemian Club, became famous in conspiracy research circles as mentioned earlier when Alex Jones infiltrated and recorded the dark rituals being held there. Kathy recalls being tortured there. Specifically, she recalls being at Bohemian Grove, aged five, tied to a stone altar

---

12 https://douglasdietrich.com/2019/11/01/child-abuse-at-the-presidio-the-parents-agony-the-armys-coverup-the-prosecutions-failure/

surrounded by three hooded figures who were trying to 'steal her soul.' Kathy remembers them saying "We can't break her," however she believes she did lose some of her soul that day. (Later on during her recovery process of soul retrieval, she recalled fragments of her being from this and other traumas.) Kathy was forced to watch a child sacrifice at Bohemian Grove. In the end, she only escaped because her father died. Her multiple traumas led her to suffer from TMJ (Temporal Manipular Joint) Disorder, which causes great pain in the head, making it hard for those with it to think.

Kathy managed to heal herself through self-love and self-work; how she did it is described in chapter 18.

Chapter 8 – The Testimony of Paul Bonacci

Like most SRA victims, Paul Bonacci has been through unspeakable horrors and managed to survive. What makes Bonacci different is that he successfully sued his handlers. In this legal deposition[13], he recalls how he was programmed to have at least 18 alters. He grew up in an orphanage home for boys. He was prostituted as part of the Franklin Child Prostitution Ring to high level politicians and celebrities. Bonacci was one of the most important witnesses in the Franklin Cover-up as exposed in the 1992 book entitled *The Franklin Cover-up: Child Abuse, Satanism, and Murder in Nebraska*[14] by former Nebraska state senator John DeCamp.

Like some of the other SRA victims discussed in this book (Kathy Collins, Cathy O'Brien and Fiona Barnett), he was taken to

---

13 https://www.youtube.com/watch?v=QuiBsh_Yq2E

14 https://www.amazon.com/Franklin-Cover-up-Satanism-Murder-Nebraska/dp/0963215809

Bohemian Grove. He specifically identified Hunter S. Thompson there, and said that he saw him participating in a game with a group of men that involved hunting down and killing children in the woods, with firearms. He recalls President George Bush Sr. being involved.

Like Kathy Collins, Bonacci was part of called Project Monarch. In case you were wondering about why the name 'monarch' was chosen for this program, here is a good explanation[15]:

The name MONARCH is not necessarily defined within the context of royal nobility, but rather refers to the monarch butterfly. When a person is undergoing trauma induced by electroshock, a feeling of light-headedness is evidenced; as if one is floating or fluttering like a butterfly. There is also a symbolic representation pertaining to the transformation or metamorphosis of this beautiful insect: from a caterpillar to a cocoon (dormancy, inactivity), to a butterfly (new creation) which will return to its point of origin. Such is the migratory pattern that makes this species unique.

Interestingly enough, Paul says that Monarch was a US Military program to create spies – and also to potentially take over the US

[15] https://archive.org/details/CIAandProjectMonarchFullHistoryRonPatton

Federal Government. He lists the 6 different categories he came across (which are similar to what is described in the previous chapter, but a little different):

– Class A alters live day-to-day, relatively normal lives;
– Class B alters have never fully grown up, so perform activities accompanied by a person (their handler);
– Class C alters have only partial personalities, and are used for one direct purpose only;
– Class D alters are those split from other alters, but can't handle normal activities. They are very disturbed;
– Class E alters are in control of other alters, and have triggers in place to set up activation of abilities or disabilities; and
– Class F alters are very small alters. Some have triggers. Their sole responsibility was to ensure other alters were on time.

Children are used because they can easily dissociate. This means the handlers could hide themselves – if a child or victim was captured, one alter could not remember what the other alter did or experienced, thus couldn't reveal the secrets. Alters don't recall what they did.

Paul was trained as a child to be a male prostitute, to seduce and perform sexual acts with people in positions of power, so they could be compromised, then bribed or blackmailed. He also received training on how to "photograph documents with his mind" to be later relayed to his handlers. He said there was a plan for him to become an ambassador in Germany, then return to the US to become an elected official.

He names Army Reserve Colonel Michael Aquino as his main controller or handler, who was also the leader of the Temple of Set and involved in human sacrifice. He also names Bill Plemmons and Gary Ackerman as Monarch handlers. Some of training happened at Offutt AFB (Nebraska) and Fort Riley (Kansas), but much at the Presidio Child Day Care Center as mentioned in chapter 7. Paul was programmed beginning in 1974 and ending roughly in 1980, but says his programming broke down in 1986. He was arrested and went to jail in 1988-89.

He says that many of the handlers are Satanists, but not all.

Finally, to conclude this chapter, here is a quote[16] from the aforementioned DeCamp book that describes what Paul was forced to do:

• *Picking up cash in exchange for drugs at various Tennessee locations. Bonacci identifies several country music personalities as contacts.*

---

[16] https://igoychuk.wordpress.com/2021/01/10/conspiracy-theory-or-a-real-conspiracy/

• Trips on behalf of the North American Man-Boy Love Association (NAMBLA), the pedophile group now given semiofficial status by the United Nations. Paul cites travel to the Netherlands and Germany carrying child pornography for subsequent "import" to the U.S.A. to avoid prosecution. In Amsterdam, he names "Charles Hester," and the British "Tommie Carter," who had on computer a global list of child pornography users. NAMBLA is also cited for organizing auctions of children.

• Travel to Hawaii, New York, Washington (in connection with Craig Spence) to compromise public figures by performing homosexual pedophile sex with them.

• The trip to California where [a] boy was ritually murdered, accompanied by "Monarch" contact, Mark Johnson of Denver, Colorado,

• Travel to Mexico for the transportation of drugs, guns, and children. Paul was accompanied by the gangster-figure "Emilio," who otherwise directed the kidnapping of Johnny Gosch of Des Moines, Iowa. Johnny Gosch's parents commend Paul Bonacci as an accurate witness relative to that crime.

• Training under "Captain Foster" (survival skills) at Fort Riley, Kansas, under "Lt. Dave Bannister" (intelligence) at Fort Bragg, North Carolina, under "Col. Harris Livik" at Fort Defiance, Virginia, who is said to run a military school and to have housed "Monarch" boys. "Col. Bill Risher" of Bamberg, South Carolina, is said to have supplied children for Michael Aquino.

• Travel to Dresden in communist East Germany, where weapons were inspected. There and in the Federal Republic of Germany, the "Monarch" personnel were frequently neo-Nazis. This milieu is a special project of Lt. Col. Aquino, who was a West European adviser to the U.S. Chiefs of Staff. Paul Bonacci has extensive experience in the Aryan Nation and other White Supremacist cults. An account of the origin of the "Monarch" project has been compiled by those who have been debriefing MPD child-victims. Nazi experimentation in World War II concentration camps were said to have gone beyond simply insane physical tortures. They brainwashed people, for military and strategic purposes. After the war, Allen Dulles and other Western intelligence people brought Nazi doctors out for use in the United States. A teenaged concentration camp inmate named Greenbaum, who had participated to save himself, also came to the United States. Known later as "Dr. Green," he became a

high-level brainwasher, and is widely represented in brainwashing programs with a distinctive Cabalistic magic theme. The precise details of these horrors lie deeply buried in national security archives. But this history, as told to psychiatrists, dovetails with what is definitively known about Anglo-American intelligence operations and the German Nazis. And once again, the story goes right back to Nebraska. The killers in the Nazi camps were themselves trained and organized by psychiatrists and eugenicists, operating from the "T4" bureau. These psychiatrists had long been the pets of white supremacist British and American financier networks. At least some of these Nazi doctors were spirited out of Germany under the supervision of former Bank of England Governor Montagu Norman and Tavistock Institute Director John R. Rees on behalf of the British government. Norman, personally an insane Theosophist who had been chief of the prewar pro-Nazi faction within England, and Rees organized postwar propaganda and continuing psychological warfare activities, and created "Orwellian" groupings within U.S. psychiatry and mental health fields."

Chapter 9 – The Testimony of Ronald Bernard

Ronald Bernard, a Dutch man, is a fascinating whistleblower and a man who extricated himself from the dark Satanic world before he got in too deep – but he was in deep enough to get a very good understanding of just how real and horrific it was.

As alluded to in chapter 1, when Ronald entered the world of high banking as a younger man, he was told that in order to succeed, he would need to put his conscience deep in the freezer or on ice (meaning he would have to suppress it, and do things that ordinary people connected to their conscience would not do). Step by step, as he gained the trust of his employers and showed that he could get his job done, ruthlessly if needed, he began to get invited to the outer level of Satanic ritual events. He reveals how he was initially invited to rituals with naked women, first as a spectator, but then as a participant. Afterwards, he was invited to participate in Satanic sacrifice – at which point he quit, broke down, was tortured to maintain secrecy but escaped to become a whistleblower. The invitation to participate in the Satanic sacrifice of children was the trigger that reawakened his conscience. Part of his breakdown included winding up at a hospital in intensive care, having an NDE (Near Death Experience) and even an OBE (Out of Body Experience).

Ronald learnt many things from his ordeal. He discovered that, by his estimate, there are around 8,000 to 8,500 people running the entire world. He exposes how the goal of this of inner circle of manipulators was to build a worldwide dictatorship (the New World Order). He talks about the accuracy of The Protocols of the Learned Elders of Zion, why the 6 million figure given for the Holocaust is fake, the end goal of the Freemasons (to rebuild the Temple of Solomon in Jerusalem) and how cryptos were created by the intelligence agencies (the NSA in 1996 was already describing something like a cryptocurrency in this report[17]).

---

[17] groups.csail.mit.edu/mac/classes/6.805/articles/money/nsamint/nsamint.htm

Since he was privy to the secrets of the Satanic ruling class, he also describes the structure of the NWO. It is dominated by central banking, composed of banks that are essentially "free states" with full legal and juristic immunity. The BIS (Bank of International Settlements) is on top and is inviolable; next comes the IMF and World Bank, then the central banks of Europe, US, etc. (all still above national governments). Finally come the regular banks, stock market centers, etc. The whole system is designed to siphon money out of society from the poor up to the rich. This ties in with what we know from other sources of evidence, e.g. that the 'City of London' is not part of the UK nor the EU, but is its own entity and jurisdiction[18].

Importantly, Ronald learnt that the wealthy elite act like they're on opposite sides but secretly work together to suppress the masses so it doesn't get too crowded at the top. They are psychopathic parasites who view the planet as a resource to be squeezed. Or, more accurately, as he says in this interview[19]:

This is not about humans; this is about a very evil dark force that enjoys destroying all life on this planet.

---

18 https://twitter.com/ofpeace1974/status/1708480015560577357

19 https://www.bitchute.com/video/gnxTfFuX7Not/

Chapter 10 – The Testimony of Cathy O'Brien

Like the other survivors in this book, Cathy O'Brien is an incredibly brave person. She underwent some especially torturous and cruel experiences. She's from the US and grew up in Michigan. She released a 1995 book called *Trance Formation of America*[20] which details what she endured. Here is a short section from her website[21]:

In 1995 when the US National Security Act was invoked on her testimony for US Congressional Permanent Select Committees on Intelligence Oversight, that testimony was released through her book TRANCE Formation of America, written with Mark Phillips. As detailed in TRANCE, Cathy became a 'candidate' for MK Ultra mind control due to a dissociative disorder developed from incest. Cathy's pedophile

---

[20] https://www.amazon.com/Trance-Formation-America-Cathy-OBrien/dp/0966016548

[21] https://trance-formation.com/about-mark-and-cathy/

father Earl O'Brien sold her into MK Ultra due to his illicit connections into a local Michigan Mafia child pornography ring sanctioned by local politician Gerald Ford. As Ford's political career escalated to heading the Warren Commission that covered up the Kennedy Assassination and to becoming President of the US, Cathy's victimization rose proportionately.

Through systematic torture and well documented NASA/military mind control programming, Cathy was forced to do the "unthinkable" and participate in CIA Black Ops and White House/Pentagon level operations during the Reagan/Bush Administration.

In 1988, intelligence insider Mark Phillips rescued Cathy and her then 8-year-old daughter, Kelly. Using methods gained in mind sciences, he taught Cathy how to remember what she'd been programmed to forget and reclaim control over her own mind and life.

Cathy was a former victim of MK Ultra mind control. MK Ultra began in 1953 with newly CIA-recruited scientists and technicians escorted out of Nazi Germany at the end of WWII via Operation Paperclip. MK Ultra was a well-funded and wide-ranging project that was attempting to unlock the secrets of the human mind and control it. The MK stands for 'mind kontrolle' or mind control using the German word for 'control' indicating the Nazi presence. As mentioned earlier, MK Ultra had 149 subprojects[22], some of which included using hypnosis, LSD and magic mushrooms on people to see how susceptible they would become to programming. For instance, here was the stated aim of some of the projects:

Subproject 23: Synthesize new drugs and modify old ones to determine their effectiveness in modifying behavior.

Subproject 26: ... develop significant keys to hypnotic susceptibility which may be adaptable to field use.

Subproject 73: Establish whether susceptibility to hypnosis can be increased by use of drugs, such as alcohol, mescaline, scopolamine, LSD, etc. Also, to determine the extent to which various drugs possess specific "hypnosis-like" effects.

Cathy was programmed to become a sex slave and was repeatedly abused and raped by 'esteemed' figures such as George Bush Sr., Dick Cheney, Bill Clinton, Hillary Clinton, Gerald Ford, George Romney (Mitt's father) and other figures inside the Mormon Church.

A theme that occurred with Cathy and other SRA victims (like Brice Taylor, chapter 12) is that she had a daughter called Kelly who was

---

22 https://www.illuminatirex.com/list-of-mkultra-subprojects/

also, as mentioned above, brought under mind control and into the Satanic world as a sex slave. It is possible that these little girl so-called 'Bush Babies' are mostly or all named Kelly. Despite the horrifying trauma that both Cathy and Kelly experienced at the hands of these serial rapists and murderers, they managed to escape alive and undo the layers of sex slave programming.

Chapter 11 – The Testimony of Chantal Frei

Chantal Frei (a pseudonym) is another SRA survivor from Europe. She grew up in Switzerland, and was only six years old when the Satanists decided to make her into a 'Mother of Darkness' – a rank which is one of the most senior positions within the Satanic cult (this will be discussed further in chapter 15 where Jessica Czebotar revealed the same thing happened to her). In interviews[23] like this, Chantal reveals the reason why the cult selected her for this role: they considered her to be strong enough because she had survived being hunted. That's right; Chantal, like other SRA survivors, was forced as a young child to participate in a Satanic human hunting ritual where she, and the other children around her, were literally hunted to death. In Chantal's case, she was hunted on the grounds of the Belgian castle Chateau des Amerois ("Mothers of Darkness" Castle – see chapter 17). Chantal says she had a 'break' in her programming in 2006 (at age 35).

---

23 https://www.bitchute.com/video/5lXQbK4f6kF6/

In her book *SPEAKING OUT!: My Life Under and Escape From Satanic Ritual Abuse*[24], Chantal reveals what happens inside the Satanic world. Here is an excerpt[25] about the human hunting game:

When I was about six years old, I was taken to a summer camp in Belgium. It was held at Amerois Castle ... We children had to strip naked there. We were all given a pair of flat, brown-beige shoes and had to put them on. Then we went into the forest. There was a hunting game. There were many deer, dogs and hunters. The role of us kids was to play the deer. We were chased naked through the forest. I remember being terrified. So I ran for my life ... I heard gunshots and children screaming in the forest ... The little boy, who called himself Marc, showed me a big pile of leaves and told me to hide in there ... That was my salvation ... My right thigh hurt badly and blood was running down my thigh. I had been shot ... My survival was celebrated, as was Marc's. The celebration consisted of sex. Sex with adults. Sex with animals, and then finally sex between me and Marc. A rod was

---

[24] https://www.amazon.com/SPEAKING-OUT-Escape-Satanic-Ritual/dp/B0B5KV4FSZ

[25] https://www.newsfox.com/news/20220823022

stuck into his penis, and he was ordered to penetrate me ... In this state of pain and complete confusion, I was asked if I would do everything they expected of me in the future. In return, they would give me life.

In this interview[26], Chantal speaks out about her experiences as a survivor of ritual abuse and mind control. Her account is revealing and consistent with that of other survivors. She met with celebrities, heads of state and European royalty. She was taken to well-known places (both known publicly and known to be associated with Satanism), including the White House, secret military facilities, the aforementioned Chateau des Amerois and a famous Spanish basilica or church called La Sagrada Familia in Barcelona. These places are the same ones mentioned by other survivors, although Chantal is the only survivor in this book to mention La Sagrada Familia. There, she helped to lead a ceremony known as 'Satan's Wedding' where a pregnant woman was sacrificed for Satan's honor. Chantal had to kill this woman. The 'wedding feast' included the Satanists eating human flesh and drinking human blood like a Christian mass communion, except with real flesh and blood. Chantal states that in the Satanic

---

[26] https://web.archive.org/web/20220826175357/https://www.youtube.com/watch?v=FiV72IL8cy0

world, they celebrate April 30th as Satan's Birthday.

Many famous people were in attendance; some wore hoods, some were naked. The people in attendance included Prince Philip, former UK PM Tony Blair, French rugby union player Serge Blanco, French actor Gerard Depardieu, actress Elizabeth Chiu and 3 tenor singers including Pavarotti (who was not yet established or famous at the time) who were on the stage. Interestingly, Chantal reveals that Lady Diana was there, under the control of Dodi's father Mohammad El-Fayed. Chantal had the impression that Diana was forced to be there, and was guarded while she was there. Chantal was repeatedly raped in public on the altar right next to the sacrificed dead body, with the poor woman's blood getting all over her. Afterwards, there was a party with orgies where Chantal was also raped.

She met Bill and Hillary Clinton at similar events. She attended events at the White House. She met former UK Queen Elizabeth and was abused by former US President Jimmy Carter. She recalls being dressed by former UK PM Margaret Thatcher. On another occasion, she was delivered to Tom Cruise in a birdcage as a birthday present to him, and underwent a ritual where she was forced to kill adult men. She said he enjoyed this.

She also reveals[27]:

I do not remember how many child sacrifices I had to take part in until I finished my 'training'. However, I still remember one very clearly. It took place in Six-Fontaines VD in Switzerland ... Both of us were the same age: about eight years old ... The flesh of dead children, which was then consumed and shared as a 'body'. In this way I had to celebrate with Satanists their 'communion'. The body and blood had to be as innocent as possible. A Satanic supper for the glory of Satan, their god.

Satanism is all about inversion and opposites; remember, the word 'Satan' itself means 'opposer.' Chantal reveals that Satanic holidays are celebrated on Christian holidays, but with the reverse meaning.

Chantal remembers lots of little details about her programming and about the Satanic cult. She alludes to how each color symbolizes something specific in the Satanic world; for example, she remembers a 'yellow trigger' where she was punished and that 'purple' meant she and the other children had to stay silent. She also recalls butterfly symbolism being used. As a younger child, she was abused by teenagers and adults. This is a feature of the system: those on top abuse

---

27 https://www.newsfox.com/news/20220823022

those below, all the way throughout the hierarchy. When she reached a certain age, she had to act as a mother in a very perverse way: she had to teach the new young girls educated into the cult what she had been taught – to prepare their bodies in such a way that, when they were later sexually abused, no trace would be left behind, or that few traces as possible would be left behind.

Chantal says the Satanic cult is connected to a cult of sun worshippers, although from my research, I believe it is one and the same cult (the late Jordan Maxwell in his research such as in his video *Dawn of a New Day*[28] showed how the symbolism of the rising sun has cropped up throughout history across many cultures as one of the most fundamental occult symbols of all). Chantal reveals how, inside the Satanic world, everything is sexual; they combine sex with everything; there is an absolute obsession over it. Also, in the Satanic world, it's like a contest: the more perverted you are, the higher you go in the hierarchy. Finally, Chantal states that the Satanists acted like they did because they believed they were getting their power from Satan.

---

[28] https://www.bitchute.com/video/pw0CCi4sNusC/

DeesIllustration.com

Chapter 12 – The Testimony of Brice Taylor

In going public, Brice Taylor was helped by former FBI agent Ted Gunderson. At the time of his retirement, after completing a 27 year career, he was Senior Special Agent in charge of the Los Angeles division, with over 700 agents under his command. He was a qualified forensic expert on cults and SRA, and testified in court on the topics. In this video[29], Gunderson stated that *"Brice Taylor's story has been confirmed over and over again through [numerous] sources. I also have contacts on the inside the US Intelligence Community. I have information from various sources that judges, law enforcement, prosecutors, attorneys, doctors and many prominent individuals, including actors, actresses, football players, baseball players, are involved in these type of activities."*

Before his death, and in the same video, Gunderson estimated there were 4 million practicing Satanists in the USA. According to

---

[29] https://www.youtube.com/watch?v=zhl01wQm7sg

him, Brice Taylor was one of the highest level healed survivors of MK Ultra trauma-based mind control ever to go public.

Brice (real name Susan Ford) explains[30] how her pedophile father allowed the programming to be done through sexual abuse and Satanic abuse. She recalls how she was forced to witness animals being sacrificed. Her church was a cover for pornography and child prostitution. She was also programmed at military bases. For torturing, they used drugs, mental and physical torture, sensory deprivation, light and sound technology (e.g. shining a bright light in someone's eyes), 'splitting' (saying two different things simultaneously into each ear, one loud, one soft, etc.), electroshock and frequency technology.

Brice tells how she was 'owned' by actor and comedian Bob Hope (who died in 2003) – i.e. that she was 'bought' in a sex slave auction which are apparently common in the world of Satanism. She reveals how both Hope and Henry Kissinger (who died at the age of 100 right before this book was published) were her handlers or programmers. She was mainly programmed to be a presidential sex slave, however this also included being prostituted out to other top politicians and celebrities. She was programmed to wear

---

30 https://web.archive.org/web/20140520145155/https://www.youtube.com/watch?v=Cb3KTQyP3zE

diamonds so top officials would know she was a presidential sex slave.

In addition to this, she was also programmed to be a courier. She was involved in remote viewing and telepathic experiments; she could read people's minds. She reveals how Kissinger would get sex slaves like Brice to impart messages to world leaders after sex, when they were in a more receptive state. Brice was programmed to have a photographic memory. She spied for Kissinger by going to the files of top officials, to read and record them, then report the contents back to Kissinger. She was also used as a drug runner; Brice has stated in her presentations and interviews that the US Government is primarily backed by drugs and guns.

Brice authored the 1999 book *Thanks for the Memories: The Truth has Set Me Free!*[31] where she names the names. She was forced to have sex with US Governors, Presidents, celebrities and other world leaders. She exposes how she was raped by:

---

[31] https://www.amazon.com/Thanks-Memories-memoirs-Kissingers-mind-controlled-ebook/dp/B0B194B6DX

- US President John Kennedy
- US President Lyndon Johnson
- US President Richard Nixon
- US President Gerald Ford
- US President Jimmy Carter
- US President George Bush Sr.
- Prince Philip
- King (but then Prince) Charles
- Bob Hope
- Henry Kissinger
- Nelson Rockefeller
- Alan Greenspan
- Elvis Presley
- Sammy Davis Jr.

She says she was brought to Rockefeller mansions to have sex with Prince Philip, Prince (now King) Charles and family members of the Kennedy bloodline. She was taken to Las Vegas "on assignment," watched by Frank Sinatra, to be prostituted to people like Elvis Presley (she watched in horror as he would throw up because he was programmed) and Sammy Davis Jr. She says she was made to film pornography with dolphins with Sylvester Stallone.

Because she moved in inside circles, she saw many secrets. She reveals how entertainers like Neal Diamond and Michael Jackson were programmed, how Alan Greenspan (one of her rapists and former head of the US Federal Reserve, the private banking cartel) would control things at the Federal Reserve so that when drug money flowed in, it would look normal and unsuspicious. She also reveals how Hope and Kissinger would already research everything they needed to know about certain people, then invite them to parties where there were drugs, sex slaves and kids etc., in order to blackmail them or enlist them in the NWO. She says that most US Presidents were 33rd Degree Masons, and that Masons and Shriners were the top Secret Societies involved in abusing her. She both overheard and was told that all wars, stock market crashes and other crises were intentionally caused. She reveals how Kissinger and Nelson Rockefeller would discuss the strategy of hiding all this out in the open – that big secrets were best protected by pubic incredulity. This idea is echoed in a phrase attributed to Hitler's propagandist Joseph Goebbels: "If you tell a lie big enough and keep repeating it, people will eventually come to believe it. The lie can be maintained only for such time as the State can shield the people from the political, economic and/or military consequences of the lie. It thus becomes vitally important for the State to use all of its powers to repress dissent, for the truth is the mortal enemy of the lie, and thus by extension, the truth is the greatest enemy of the State."

Brice makes the comment that mind control – whether on an individualized, scientific level through MK Ultra techniques, or on a collective, propagandistic level through mass media programming – is one of the major weapons of the NWO controllers.

Her handlers had sophisticated program themes, but used them for all victims, so that now SRA survivors can recognize each other by certain key phrases or themes: Wizard of Oz, over the rainbow, dolphins and whales, hearts and roses, Monarch butterflies, etc. Like other mind control victims, she was programmed to fall asleep or get sick if she started remembering her programming.

The Satanic agenda is bound up with pedophilia. Brice was programmed to recruit and lure young kids into cars, where they would be taken from their parents, used in pornography films and for SRA, then killed. She was instructed to bring her own children to the military bases to be programmed also. This brings us to her daughter Kelly. In a chapter of her book called "Baby Monarchs Are Born," Brice writes that while Reagan was president, then Vice President George Bush, a serial pedophile, rapist, murderer and Satanist, made her daughter into a so-called Bush Baby with the name of Kelly (a theme introduced in chapter 10 with Cathy O'Brien):

"Over the years, Kelly was closely tied into the trauma I received ... *Repeatedly she was tortured and traumatized in front of me in an effort to keep me in line. Her torture fragmented her psyche in order to create multiple personalities within her, so she could follow in my footsteps for later use as a 'presidential model.' Unfortunately she didn't have to wait very long for that so-called 'privilege' as our newly elected vice president at the time, George Bush, was/is a pedophile and Kelly was created to be, as I later found out from a renegade CIA operative, what was called a 'Bush Baby.'"*

Like other SRA victims (such as Bonacci [chapter 8] and O'Brien [chapter 10]), Brice recounts being hunted. The human hunting theme is another horrific but common Satanic theme. In Brice's case, she recalls being hunted by George Bush on Bob Hope's ranch.

Brice also reveals that, at one time, then President Ronald Reagan took her to meet Queen Elizabeth. She overheard them talking about Brice's genetic structure and bloodline. The queen was very interested in having Reagan be the father of a child to be carried by Brice. They decided she would be impregnated for later breeding within the royal family.

Finally, I will end this chapter with a telling revelation from Brice. She reveals how, as a message courier, she was programmed to overhear conversations and report them back to Kissinger. Guess what Kissinger would do that information? He would in turn report it back to his superiors, the mysterious Satanic "Council" (discussed more in the following chapters).

This Council was/is above US Presidents, above the late Kissinger and above everyone – it rules the world. Brice states that Kissinger, when he was alive, was the top dog as far as the Council was concerned, because he had the mind they needed to carefully and effectively strategize plans far in advance. Kissinger usually got the results they wanted. In the Council's eyes, Rockefeller was more dispensable because although he had money and power, he didn't have the mastermind Kissinger had. Brice writes:

"Behind the scenes, Henry controlled decisions and actions taken by the State Department in matters of foreign relations always attempting to bring about a situation where the Council was in total control globally. They saw it as a game, a lifelong plan, with the outcome hopefully being that finally this generation of the global elite would succeed in the game that their forefathers had not been able to pull off. It created ambition and drive among them."

This explains why Kissinger was around for so many decades at the very top level of American and world politics. In many realms and industries, people get ahead or advance up the career ladder according primarily to their rank in the Satanic hierarchy, not some other hierarchy. Even in his last year of life, Kissinger at 100 years old was still able to meet with powerful foreign leaders such as

Chinese President Xi Jinping (as occurred in July 2023), when at that time the Chinese were still refusing to meet with the current US President (Joe Biden) and only (grudgingly) met the current US Secretary of State (Antony Blinken).

Chapter 13 – The Testimony of Fiona Barnett

Fiona Barnett is another incredibly courageous woman who went through the depths of hell. Her experience and testimony is very similar to Cathy O'Brien's and Brice Taylor's, except that Cathy and Brice are from America while Fiona is from Australia. She exposes the same themes: CIA child trafficking, MK Ultra mind control, international VIP pedophile rings (which are all connected), SRA and Satanic rituals involving rape and sacrifice. Her testimony corroborates Cathy's and Brice's in so many ways; Fiona names the same names (e.g. she exposes how was also raped by former US President Richard Nixon on a plane, and had to be stitched up by military doctor).

In her 450+ page book *Eyes Wide Open*[32], Fiona exposes in massive detail the Australian pedophile rings and Satanic groups currently in operation. She names famous actors, celebrities, judges and politicians, including several former

[32] https://ia803208.us.archive.org/10/items/eyeswideopen-2020-edition/EWO_June2020_LockdownEdition.pdf

Australian prime ministers and one former US president (Nixon) who personally sexually abused her. Her press conference on October 22nd, 2015 in Sydney received widespread mainstream media attention.

To summarize Fiona's story, she recalls having had flashbacks to ages two and three where she was abused and sexually assaulted by Antony Kidman, father of famous Australian actress Nicole Kidman. She was taken to parties, dropped off by herself, instructed to say "starchild is here" and then allow famous cocaine-snorting politicians, actors and celebrities to rape her – after which they pretended to drown her in the pool. She reveals that Nicole Kidman was a victim of the ring too, and was in the room when her father Antony killed someone, but covered it up. Fiona claims Nicole was a "bitch," didn't care about her (Fiona) and, when Fiona's story broke in December 2015, hired security guards to stalk Fiona using a "scientology approach" to nearly cause an "accident." Fiona says her handlers used cattle-prodding electroshock to cause her disassociation.

Overall, she explains how Australia received a large number of Nazi war criminals, such as her own step-grandparents, which mirrors the way in which top Nazi scientists and technicians were secretly exported to Western nations like the US at the end of WWII in Operation Paperclip (as mentioned earlier). She reveals that many Australian leaders were offspring of these Nazi criminals; they are the bloodlines who were born into Satanism and SRA. According to her, every organization in Australia has been infiltrated: hospitals, psychiatry, politics and child advocacy groups, with CPS (Child Protective Services) being nothing more than a pedophile protection racket. While the US has two extremes (secular and degenerate Hollywood materialism vs. Bible loving Christianity), Fiona states that Australia has only one extreme (pedophilia). She perceives Australia as socialist and CIA run, a test case for programs happening elsewhere. She exposes how the CIA is behind the pedophilia network in Australia and worldwide, including branches such as the OTO, the Eastern Star, the Freemasons, Scientology, the Catholic Church and the Australian military.

She describes the NWO pyramid as she has experienced it:

Top Level: Insider VIPs (perpetrating Satanic Ritual Abuse)
Next Level: Ordinary pedophiles (without Satanism)
Next Level: Recruits from private schools
Next Level: The Mafia
Next Level: Gangs

She highlights that only pure bloodliners can make it to the top, and that there are only 12 or 13 bloodlines at the very top, who the underlings revere as demigods. The 300 or so bloodlines below that can never make it to the top. There is some very important information to come on bloodlines in the next chapter, however for now, this is in line with what other researchers such as Fritz Springmeier and David Icke have discovered. Springmeier wrote a book entitled *13 Bloodlines of the Illuminati*[33] where he claims the 13 are comprised of the Astor Bloodline, the Bundy Bloodline, the Collins Bloodline, the DuPont Bloodline, the Freeman Bloodline, the Kennedy Bloodline, the Li Bloodline, the Onassis Bloodline, the Reynolds Bloodline, the Rockefeller Bloodline, the Rothschild Bloodline, the Russell Bloodline and the Van Duyn Bloodline. Icke has exposed in his research the consistent theme that, among the bloodline families, they strive to keep their genetics pure by controlling who their offspring marry, and that this desire is not snobbishness but rather directly related to the amount of reptilian DNA in their blood which they seek to preserve at all costs (see next chapter). This could well be the basis of the mindset that rulers have had throughout the ages that they have 'the divine right to rule' – i.e. that this mindset stems from a certain reptilian genetic heritage because it influences such thinking.

---

33 https://www.amazon.com/Bloodlines-Illuminati-1-Fritz-Springmeier/dp/1796271500

At a young age, Fiona was introduced by her own family to an international child trafficking pedophile ring based in Sydney. Some victims are kidnapped off the street, some are bred for it (without having birth certificates) and some are brought into it through multi-generational abuse, then expected and trained to become the new perpetrators and administrators of it. Despite being Australian, Fiona suffered a lot of abuse in the US, such as being taken after-dark pedophile parties at Disneyland and to the infamous Bohemian Grove secret society where she was codenamed 'Candy Girl' and forced to participate in a child rape hunt party. She also reports witnessing cannibalism, having seen some of her molesters keeping a frozen girl hanging on a meat hook, and eating sacrificed human flesh in front of her.

Fiona has a lot to say about the dark underbelly of Australia. She lauds former NSW politician Franca Arena, who stood up in 1996 in Parliament under parliamentary privilege and declared that there was a large pedophile ring involving politicians, judges and doctors. She accused Commissioner Wood of covering up the Royal Commission investigation he led. Fiona further adds that commissions and investigations like this often create a 'False Memory Foundation' which is a fake organization set up by pedophiles. Fiona states there were orgy parties at Parliament House, which echoes what goes on at the White House in the US and Westminster in the UK.

Perhaps the most shocking part of Fiona's testimony is her recollection of an event she was forced to participate in at Bathurst (rural NSW) in 1985. The link is somehow still live on YouTube here[34] however it also preserved here[35] on the Wayback Machine internet archive. At the 23-minute mark, Fiona describes how she was 15 years old and surrounded in a room full of cops, priests from St. Stanislaus College, Australian actor Bruce Spence, former Australian cricket captain Richie Benaud, former NSW police commissioner John Avery and former Australian senior politician Kim Beazley Sr. They proceeded to perform a black magic ritual which involved sacrifice and rape.

Fiona has done an astonishing job connecting the dots of this whole topic. She references other whistleblowers (like Ronald Bernard from chapter 9), other SRA victims (Kathleen Sullivan[36]), detectives or policemen who investigated this (James Rothstein) and

---

34 https://www.youtube.com/watch?v=soZpqrCji5c

35 https://web.archive.org/web/20230314164534/https://www.youtube.com/watch?v=soZpqrCji5c

36 https://www.goodreads.com/en/book/show/874586

of course some of the pedophiles and child traffickers themselves. Here is a partial list. Many on this list personally abused and raped her:

– Bill Clinton (former US president)
– Hillary Clinton (former US secretary of state)
– Keith Raniere (NXIVM. Fiona says NXIVM is MK-Ultra)
– Allison Mack (NXIVM)
– Billy Graham (evangelist)
– Walt Disney (founder of Disneyland. Fiona was taken to pedophile parties there after dark, says Walt was a pedophile and says she also saw Ted Turner [founder of CNN] there)
– Elton John (musician)
– John Bell (actor)
– Bruce Spence (actor)
– Kerry Packer (Australian billionaire media mogul)
– Alan Jones (Australian radio announcer)
– Molly Meldrum (Australian TV presenter)
– Kim Beazley Sr. (former Australian politician)
– Bob Carr (former Australian politician, who with Kim Beazley Sr. above went over to Bohemian Grove to "represent" Australia on taxpayer dollars)
– Gough Whitlam (former Australian prime minister)
– Bob Hawke (former Australian prime minister)
– Paul Keating (former Australian prime minister)

– Robert Menzies (former Australian prime minister)
– John Kerr (former governor general of Australia. Fiona states that Whitlam and Kerr were homosexual lovers)

Here is a quote from her book:

Traditional high-end Satanic cults are organised like a caste system. Membership in the upper hierarchy is attainable by birth only, like the aristocracy. One can't marry or buy into the top classes. At the top of the pyramid sit the blue bloodlines headed by the Rothschilds. This ruling class is worshipped as demigods like the reverence shown for the Egyptian pharaohs. Beneath this class sit hundreds of 'mortal' family bloodlines that make up a kind of intelligentsia. This group is characterised as high IQ and are granted access to worldly success - so long as they play the game. If members of this class feel morally in conflict with the coven's activities, this usually manifests as 'mental illness,' and if they rebel against 'the family' they are disposed of. Below this ruling class sit a menagerie of coven members that constitute the anarchy. In Europe these members are bound by location. In a young country like Australia they are united by things such as nationality or interest ... Conflict exists between the traditional Satanists and the modern self-styled covens. The lowest coven groups compete amongst each other for the unattainable power and status of the hierarchy whom they jealously despise. As portrayed in Harry Potter series, the ruling classes look down upon the lower groups with contempt and view them as animalistic, annoyingly clumsy, grubby and highly dispensable. They are held in disdain because they approach tasks with aggression and brute strength, which risks exposing everybody. Their most common mistake is to put their own personal wants before the collective. Their other usual flaw is their propensity to embrace assumption and an overconfidence that stems from not having been thwarted - yet. That is the mistake people like Antony Kidman and Harry Bailey made. Like a pack of mongrel dogs, this group is rewarded for success and punished for failure. They tend to be motivated by primitive drives like sex and drugs rather than higher intellectual pursuits.

Here is another quote:

Cult members maintain a public façade of family respectability behind which they will fuck anything – males, females, kids, animals ... anything ... Female cult members are just as sexually active and perverse as the men. It is just as typical for married cult women to lust after sex with children and each other. Cult members married and had children out of their duty to produce Illuminati babies.

Chapter 14 – The Testimony of Arizona Wilder

Now that we have gone through quite a few survivor testimonies, we will move into exploring the stories of two more survivors who know (or knew) the Satanic network the best – the people who went deep inside the belly of the beast and have been able to come escape with lots of information about how it operates. David Icke interviewed Arizona Wilder (real name Jennifer Nagel [birth name], Jennifer Greene [first married name] and Jennifer Kealey [second married name]) back in 1999 and helped spread her message. He released a video[37] at that time called "Revelations Of A Mother Goddess" which you can watch for free on BitChute here[38]. Arizona also did a video presentation here[39] apparently entitled "Deceived No More" that is from some time between 2000

---

37 https://www.imdb.com/title/tt7012636/

38 https://www.bitchute.com/video/bL1qfq7TzjDh/

39 https://www.bitchute.com/video/BBtC86MaFuv8/

and 2010. She hasn't been heard of in quite some time now.

Arizona was programmed and trained to conduct Satanic ritual by Joseph Mengele a.k.a. the 'Angel of Death' from the Nazi death camps of World War II – another Nazi who was welcomed by the US after the end of WWII. She was bred before birth for the role (another theme throughout Satanism) via the bloodline of her mother's family. She had a certain level of psychic ability which the Satanists desired. She was groomed and moved into a high-up position in the Satanic hierarchy known as the 'Mother Goddess.' Arizona describes how she conducted Satanic ritual alongside some of the most famous names in the United States and the United Kingdom. She says there can only be three Mother Goddesses on the Earth at any time according to the Satanic hierarchical structures, and also three of the equivalent male position. (Note: in the next chapter we will cover Jessie Czebotar's information which differs slightly on this point. Jessie says there are five 'Mothers of Darkness' as opposed to three 'Mother Goddesses').

She was programmed at an early age. In addition to being physically assaulted and raped, she was forced to drink her own urine and eat her own feces, programmed to be anorexic and bulemic, underwent electroshock, was forced to spend time in a sensory deprivation tank, had her joints dislocated then put back into place and had her eyelids taped open. She was subjected to various kinds of harmful electrical frequencies: her genitals were electrically stimulated, tones were played to her over the phone to trigger her, DEW (Directed Energy Weapons), ELF (Extremely Low Frequencies) and other microwaves were used on her which changed the electrical activity of her brain. Later on when she could drive, she was programmed to run through a red light while driving thinking it was green.

When she was five years old, she was taken to Leningrad for psychic experiments jointly conducted by Soviet scientists and the KGB. The Soviets subjected her to near drowning in icewater on three occasions to induce Near Death Experiences for their research. As part of her programming, Arizona was taken to an underground military installation beneath Area 51. There she met cloned (manufactured) Grey aliens known as 'cybers.'

Arizona mentions that part of her programming was conducted at the UCLA parapsychological research unit under the watch of Dr. Louis Jolyon West, whose name surfaces more than once in survivor testimony related to mind control. She also reveals how the Janus Group in the NATO headquarters building in Brussels tried to control her and taught her how to psychically murder people. To understand Satanism you need to understand symbology, since Satanists are black magicians who use symbols as weapons to gain power over others. Janus is the 2-headed god of beginnings and transitions in Roman mythology, and is symbolically also associated with being duplicitous and deceptive (two-faced).

Like other mind control victims, Arizona became a 'multiple' or someone who suffered from DID. In Arizona's case, as mentioned above, her programmer Mengele. The programming often breaks down after programmer dies; Mengele died in the late 1980s. Arizona's journey into unravelling her past started when she realized she had a whole lot of missing time (the exact same phenomenon experienced by alien abductees, as explained in my book *40 Incredible Real Life Alien Abductee and Contactee Experiences – Controversial Truths Revealed Series Book 2*[40]). She also mentions how she had a Kundalini experience as part of her awakening.

At this point, we arrive at the key theme that underpins Satanism. I firmly believe you can't understand Satanism without understanding the Reptilian invasion of Earth. We must ask the question: what is the point of all the Satanic ritual – all the torture, rape, killing and blood drinking? What purpose does it serve? One answer is that it opens a portal

---

40 https://www.amazon.com/Incredible-Alien-Abductee-Contactee-Experiences-ebook/dp/B0BG6G9D4P/

or interface between this dimension here on Earth and another dimension (which people have variously called the 4th dimension, the astral dimension or the lower astral dimension), through which 2-way communication can take place. The humans here can communicate their wishes to the beings on the other side, and get or take things from them, and likewise, the beings on the other side (which some would call 'gods') can communicate or implant things in this world, such as ideas in people's minds, and take things from here. This phenomenon is often called demonic possession since, during the ritual, the Satanists are in an altered state and thus highly suggestible to ideas. The term 'loosh' is sometimes used to describe the emotions harvested by these beings when they feed on humans' low vibrational states such as anxiety, anger, terror and – most of all – fear. As it turns out, these gods are the gods of yore, the ones in mythology and history who have demanded sacrifice (e.g. of firstborn children) like the 'Yahweh' of the Old Testament. This arrangement may seem to be mutually beneficial, i.e. the Satanists get power from their gods or demons in the 4th dimension, and the gods get their loosh. However, it resembles a master-slave relationship where the human Satanists give away their power, open themselves up to devilish energy and allow themselves to be controlled by it. Many artists (especially Hollywood celebrities) have made reference to this over the years, including Bob Dylan with his allusion to the idea[41] that he sold his soul to the devil.

However, another answer to this key question regarding the purpose of Satanic ritual is that it is not purely to open up a channel between this dimension and the next; it is also to feed beings right here on Earth. That's right: we're talking about extraterrestrial or interdimensional Reptilians. According to Arizona (and she is far from the only person to have witnessed this), there is an alien race of Reptilians that have invaded planet Earth, live here underground (including in the DUMBs or Deep Underground Military Bases) and have the ability to come in and out of this dimension. They have secretly controlled humanity for thousands of years, mainly through their hybrid Reptilian-human bloodlines, which form the elite aristocracy of Europe and the elite bloodlines in the US – basically the same 13 bloodlines as revealed by Springmeier in his aforementioned book. Arizona was taught the backstory by the Mothers of Darkness as early part of her training: according to this story, Aryans came to Earth from Mars (their original planet) about 6,000 years ago, after Mars was invaded by Reptilians. From the Reptilian's point of view, blond-haired, blue-eyed people are the purest form. The Reptilians followed the Aryans to Earth 2,000 years later, masquerading as gods to fool humans into

---

41 https://www.youtube.com/watch?v=jNn72qnp6kI

obeying them. By interbreeding with select Aryans, the Reptilians created an elite bloodline that persists to this day. Once the Reptilians arrived, they began to take over, installing their hybrid bloodlines in key positions of power in politics and religion. The Reptilians seek the Aryans because apparently the Aryan's genetic structure is the most suitable for them for the purpose of interbreeding and making a hybrid bloodline. This hybrid bloodline holds its form (actually, forms – both human form and reptilian form) the best, better than other racial human genetic structures.

Since these hybrid bloodlines are actually half reptilian and half human, these can change from one form to another, under certain conditions. These alien-human hybrids maintain their human shape most of the time, but when they morph into their reptilian form, Arizona (and David Icke, and others) refer to this as "shapeshifting."

With that introduction out of the way, here is what Arizona has shared about her experiences. Remember, she was inducted into the world of Satanism not just as a minor participant but rather to be a leader of it – to be one of three Mother Goddesses to conduct Satanic ritual.

Arizona emphasizes that blood – human blood, especially menstrual blood – is the key part of the ritual for the hybrid bloodlines, because they need it to maintain their human shape, maintain their sanity and live in this world, because they are not fully of this world. Without this human blood, they naturally revert into their reptilian shape. So what's so important about this blood? Human blood has secretions in it from the pituitary and pineal glands. These secretions are like endorphins, and to the hybrid alien-humans, it's like heroin. However, not all blood is the same; what they are really desiring are certain chemicals in the blood that only get released into the blood if their victim is deadly afraid. In other words, they need terrorization of their victims before they are killed to get the secretion. This is where the term 'adrenochrome' comes in; it is a chemical compound produced by the oxidation of adrenaline (or epinephrine). As for the name, the –chrome suffix indicates a relationship to color, as pure adrenochrome is deep violet.

All of this explains the low vibrational nature of the Satanic ritual – the abuse, the hunting, the torture, leading up to the final murderous sacrifice. It's about getting the victim to release the chemicals, then stealing their blood to use as energy to sustain their form. Arizona reveals how the hybrids are addicted to blood; she states how it sends them into a frenzy and induces them to shapeshift to a reptilian form, since around the scent of blood, they can't hold their human form. Even a menstruating human woman would trigger them to shapeshift. She states that they rip into their victim, eviscerate them, eat their flesh and drink their blood; who gets what organs in what order etc. goes according to rank. Rank and hierarchy is very important to the Reptilians, which makes sense, since terrestrial reptiles like crocodiles and alligators are very territorial, and the European royal families, with all their pomp and circumstance, reflect an absolute obsession with rank.

Arizona reveals how Satanic rituals happen at least every month, every full moon, and on all 8 cardinal points of the year (Imbolc, Spring Equinox, Beltane, Summer Solstice, Lughnasa, Autumn Equinox, Samhain/ Halloween, Winter Solstice). The bloodlines have mixed Satanic and Druidic holidays together, using them as key power points to conduct ritual. They also take into account the phases of the moon, because the moon has a pronounced effect on Earth. An example of Satanic ritual on a well-know holiday is Halloween: for the Satanists, this night is about worship of Satan and the celebration of harvest – harvesting human blood.

Arizona is a fountain of knowledge when it comes to naming the names. Like Cathy O'Brien, Brice Taylor and Fiona Barnett, Arizona names many former US presidents, but she also names many European leaders and royalty, since she attended Satanic ritual both in the US and Europe. Below is a list of who Arizona names, along with those who Arizona saw shapeshipt in parentheses:

American
- Lyndon Johnson (now deceased)
- Henry Kissinger (now deceased)
- Jimmy Carter
- Ronald and Nancy Reagan (now deceased)
- George H. W. Bush (Bush Sr.) (now deceased) and his 2 sons, Jeb Bush and George W. Bush (Bush Jr.)
- Madeleine Albright
- Hillary Clinton
- Newt Gingrich
- Gerald Ford (now deceased) (shapeshifted)
- Jay Rockefeller (shapeshifts)
- Zechariah Sitchin (now deceased) (shapeshifts)
- Joseph Mengele (shapeshifts)

European
- Queen Mother (now deceased) (shapeshifted)
- Queen Elizabeth (now deceased) (shapeshifted)
- Prince Philip (now deceased) (shapeshifted)
- a former president of France
- Laurence Gardner (who wrote the 1998 article in Nexus Magazine about Star Fire[42] [menstrual blood] which was a codename for Arizona)
- Earl Spencer (brother of Princess Diana)
- King Charles (then Prince at the time when Arizona saw him) (shapeshifts)
- Princess Margaret (shapeshifts)

---

[42] https://cruinthe.tripod.com/nexus/articles/starfire1.html

– Baron Guy de Rothschild (shapeshifts)
– Tony Blair (shapeshifts)

Arizona emphasizes that although members of the Spencer family were at these Satanic rituals, she never saw Diana there (although recall in chapter 11 Chantal states she did see Diana at such a ritual, against her will). She did however overhear a conversation between Fayed and Queen Elizabeth re: Diana and Dodi, which corroborates what Chantal said.

At the Satanic ritual, Arizona describes how the Satanists would wear robes of red and purple while being naked underneath. They are introduced to each other formally as though it were a courtroom. All of them have quirks as to how they act in reptilian form, but all are cold-blooded and would kill at the drop of a hat. Arizona specifically states how they go into a frenzy, and that she personally saw members of the British Royal Family and Guy de Rothschild do this. She saw all of them eat flesh and blood, with each Satanist having their own dagger and goblet.

Arizona states that the head of the Illuminati is Pindar (a name which means 'phallus of the dragon'), a man who lives somewhere in France. She has frequently made reference to people like herself being impregnated with the seed of Pindar. She also mentions that some Reptilians materialize out of another dimension into this one during ritual. The implication here again is that Satanic ritual opens a gateway and creates a frequency match to another dimension or dimensions, so that things or creatures that are normally invisible, in the realm of the unseen, can become seen.

Arizona states that although the Reptilians are psychic, they can't enter a higher dimension than the one they are in. This is what they were utilizing Arizona for. They tried to control her psychic ability so they could steer certain outcomes to be favorable for them. At the time of the interview with Icke, and in the years in the decade of the 2000s following it, the Reptilians apparently still had plans for Arizona to return to Satanism due to her psychic ability.

Arizona believes the veil is lifting, that the time is coming when the Reptilians and their hybrid bloodlines are not going to bother hiding their real form (or perhaps will not be able to). She states that changes are occurring on Earth such that they are not able to hold their shape like they used to be able to. More and more people are seeing them shapeshift; a recent example is Juliette Bryant, interviewed on Ickonic.com[43], who saw notorious pedophile, Zionist and Mossad agent Jeffrey Epstein shapeshift in front of her. Epstein was running a massive worldwide pedophile and spying ring, one of the purposes of which was to entrap

[43] https://www.bitchute.com/video/QopKJ7dGmPwT/

politicians and leaders in illegal sexual acts with minors, catch it on video and then hold it over their heads as blackmail for the rest of their lives.

According to Arizona, they are trying to install their NWO before the veil lifts and people see them for who they are. This is a very credible theory, especially given the acceleration toward worldwide tyranny we have seen in the last few years during Operation Coronavirus (the COVID scamdemic) as I cover in my book *Break Your Chains: Exposing the Worldwide Conspiracy and Presenting the Way Out*[44].

Like Brice in a previous chapter, and like Jessica in the next chapter, Arizona reveals how these bloodlines of the Illuminati were not at the very top of the Satanic pyramidal hierarchy, that instead they answered to a Grand Druid Council of some type. We will go into the specific Satanic hierarchical structure in the following chapter.

---

44 https://www.amazon.com/Break-Your-Chains-Conspiracy-Presenting/dp/B0CCCX8NTZ

Chapter 15 – The Testimony of Jessica Czebotar

One of the best sources of how Satanism operates in today's world comes from another insider who escaped. Jessica (Jessie) Czebotar was brought into the Satanic system at a very young age. Her training began at age four when she was selected for her position: she was chosen to be the future 'Mother of Darkness' which according to her is the highest, most powerful position in the entire Satanic hierarchy. She was actually trained to take over for her grandmother as one of five Mothers of Darkness. Jessie managed to get out of the system at the age of ten so she never became the Queen Mother of Darkness.

According to Jessie, the Mothers of Darkness are the directors of the system since they allegedly talk directly with 'Satan.' Below them is the Council of 300. The structure mimics political structures with an executive branch and legislative branch, or corporate structures with a CEO and a board. Satanism is run like a giant multinational corporation. Satanism is about power – and also about death. Satanic practitioners, both female and male, physically battle for positions in the hierarchy. They may engage in naked combat, sometimes in fights to the death.

Jessie understands the international Satanic network extremely well. She first described this in an interview with Dan Duval[45]. This website[46] has a great summary of the information Jessie provided, as does this short video[47]. Here is a summary of the Satanic Illuminati network and structure according to Jessie:

– **Mothers of Darkness:** Each of these five networks has a director known as the Mother of Darkness who functions like the CEOs (Chief Executive Officers) of the 'business.' They know how the system or 'company' structure works. They supervise their quadrants domestically (in the US) and internationally. They 'talk directly to Satan/ Lucifer/The Devil' or, in other words, they take a leading role in Satanic ritual where a portal is opened between this dimension and the next, so as to allow communication, vibration transfer, frequency entrainment and demonic possession to occur. Through this ritual, they get direction, vision and instruction, or they get 'their orders' if you prefer, which they then pass to the next

---

45 https://www.youtube.com/watch?v=3ydBIn-wYP0

46 https://cathyfox.wordpress.com/2020/01/18/the-five-child-trafficking-networks-of-the-illuminati/

47 https://www.bitchute.com/video/MEMEgKi3LkMJ/

group below, the Council of 300. Across from the Mothers of Darkness is a subgroup of 5 men (known as Merlin) however Jessie doesn't seem to have as much information on them.

– Council of 300 / Druidic Council / Satanic Council: This group goes by other names too, such as Galactic Federation, Federation Alliance and the Global Alliance. There are 300 seats. This is akin to a corporate board of directors. It usually consists of men who deal with financial and business decisions. The positions are called seats and they are divided into quadrants. There are a wide range of individuals in each quadrant.

This council may or may not align with what researcher John Coleman has uncovered in his work *The Committee of 300*[48]. Brilliant conspiracy analyst David Icke has stated that many of these inner cult groups don't even have names, so as to make it very difficult for researchers to learn more about them, thus allowing them to remain shrouded in the unseen. Icke has stated that the Bilderberg Group is where the seen meets the unseen, and that although Bilderberg is a more

48 https://archive.org/details/dr.-john-coleman-the-committee-of-300

powerful group than other similar groups in the realm of the seen, it is less powerful (or less at the center of the Satanic spider web) than these groups in the Satanic unseen. Those on the Council are in positions of power in the seen world, which provides a great cover story or cover life for their real activities. These positions of power include banking, politics, business, the United Nations or European Councils. Each quadrant has bloodline family representation, e.g. a head of the Van Duyn family or a head of the Rothschild family.

The job of the Council of 300 is to receive orders from the Mothers of Darkness, and they in turn give instructions to the Grand High Priestesses.

– Grand High Priestesses / Priests: These are the people at the level just below the Council of 300. Their job is to ensure the system is operating correctly within specific quadrants.

Jessie names several people at this level:

– Colonel Michael Aquino, whose name has already come up earlier in this book in relation to mind control and SRA;
– Former CIA Director John Brennan;
– Laurie Cabot Kent (a UK bloodline via the Cabot and Kent families; she was one of Jessie's top teachers); and
– Gloria Van der Bilt (mother of Anderson Cooper [CIA and CNN]) who was Grand High Priestess for the East. When one dies as Van

der Bilt did (in 2019), there is a witch's battle for the recently vacated position at the Mothers of Darkness Castle in Belgium. Such a battle takes place across many realms (physical, astral, spiritual) with physical weapons and with the use of spells (including the summoning of demons).

– High Priestess / Priests: The top eight highest ranking in the class of high priestess are able to compete for Grand High Priestess position. Their job is oversee the five departments under their jurisdiction.

– The Five Departments: There are five departments under the Priestesses. Each one is trained differently and run separately, just as compartmentalization is practiced in the military-intelligence industry, so that if one network is discovered and broken up by law enforcement, the other parts can continue. They do however cooperate. The five departments that run the Satanic networks are:

- The Mormons
- The Masons (Priory of Sion, Templars, Grand High Lodge Leaders, etc.)
- Catholic Church (including the Jesuits)
- Satanists
- The Kabbalah (Jewish mystical sect, mixed with New Age philosophies)

In addition, Nazi connections are woven all throughout the Satanic network. Some of the Jesuit priests are hidden Nazis. (I must note here that Jessie does not explain how 'Satanists' can be one of the 5 main subgroups, when the entire network is Satanic and composed of Satanists.)

The job of each department is to oversee the system's assets, namely the bloodline children (who are groomed to take on positions of power when they reach maturity) and the expendable children (who are abused and sexually exploited, then ritually killed and/or cannibalized. After this, their remains may be turned into a diamond, and their ashes sold to food companies.).

– Protectors and Assassins: Protectors are security. Each Mother of Darkness has one. The head protector runs training for the others; there are five adult protectors which guard the Mothers of Darkness, five juniors aged 12-18 who are not assigned to anyone but are kept in reserve for whomever needs protecting. There are also five children who are protectors assigned to defend the successors of the Mothers of Darkness (i.e. the people who are chosen early in their lives to be the eventual successors). They battle amongst themselves for superiority by physical and astral means.

– Brides of Satan: The Brides ensure 'Satan' is happy, and what he desires happens. They can lure a person into the system. They look beautiful. They represent Satan but do not have many duties or functions.

– Sisters of Light: There are thirteen for each quadrant, in US and internationally.

– Elite Security Team: This is another group within the structure who are different to Protectors and Assassins. They apparently have the ability to cause people disease and money problems.

– The Bloodline Familes: the bloodline families underpin a lot of the Satanic structure. See page 41 for Fritz Springmeier's list of the 13 families. According to Jessie, the Bloodline Families are like board members: they supervise departments in their territory, get messages to them and oversee the underlings of the various Satanic operations and businesses (e.g. drug trafficking, child trafficking, etc.).

Jessie reaffirms that the Satanists use the MK Ultra programming described in previous chapters. She adds that the Mormons tend to use beta kitten programming. She explains that mind controlled individuals are seen as filing cabinets of many drawers, with each drawer having many files (representing the alter or split personality). Each drawer's key is guarded by a demonic spirit. These demons or spirits need to be passed in order to access the files. When they do access the file, individuals re-live the traumatic memories associated with creation of the file/alter.

So, in summary, the Satanic network operates according to hierarchy. At the apex of the pyramid are the 5 Mothers of Darkness, then the Council of 300 (of which a subcouncil is the infamous Bilderberg Group), then the Grand High Priestesses / Priests, then the High Priestess / Priests, then the five Departments and onto lower levels.

This is the unseen structure which really runs the world behind the veneer of governments and organizations in the realm of the seen which appear to be in charge (but are given their orders and have to follow the scripted agenda).

Chapter 16 – A Quick Note on the Reptilians

This book is not over, but I feel compelled to emphasize this point right here and now: there are many people who will only be able to go so far with the reptilian topic before they shut down. They may say something like, "I can understand the corruption and the coverup ... the abuse and the human trafficking ... I see how pedophilia is related to Satanism ... I can get my mind around the rituals, sacrifice, black magic and invocations to dark deities ... but Reptilian ETs? Now that's just too much." The idea is that many people have a point at which they refuse to go any further, no matter how compelling and overwhelming the evidence is. It's a programmed knee-jerk reaction, not a thoughtful response.

I invite you to consider everything open-mindedly, do further research then make up your own mind, rather than dismissing something out of hand with not even a cursory investigation. However, my job here is to simply present the information and connect the dots; it is up to each and every reader to choose how to interpret this information, and what to take away from it.

There is no doubt that Arizona Wilder revealed incredible detail about the nature of these creatures, their hydrid bloodlines and their agenda and purpose – but she is far from the only person to have witnessed or interacted with them. Researcher David Icke presented groundbreaking information on the Reptilians, including their influence throughout thousands of years in cultures and races across the world, in his 1999 book The Biggest Secret: The Book That Will Change the World and further in his 2001 book Children of the Matrix. Others who have devoted their life to studying the reptilian phenomenon include but are not limited to:

– the late legendary alien abduction researcher Barbara Bartholic[49], who studied cattle mutilations and UFO sightings, and who used hypnosis and regression techniques with clients through which she uncovered a massive amount of information about the Reptilians. One of her protégés, James Bartley (see below) wrote the following[50] about her:

Alien Abduction Research lost a true pioneer with the passing of Barbara Bartholic. Although Barbara's work has gone largely unheralded (except amongst the many people she helped) her legacy lives on in the form of cutting edge research amongst her protégés and an understanding amongst

49 https://www.amazon.com/Barbara-Story-UFO-Investigator-Bartholic/dp/0970750773/

50 whale.to/c/legacy.html

serious researchers of the primary role played by the Reptilians in alien abductions. Barbara laid the groundwork for a deeper understanding of the Reptilian Overlordship. Indeed Barbara coined the phrase "Reptilian Overlordship." Barbara delved deeper than most abduction researchers. She didn't turn away from confronting or unsettling information. I am proud to say that I was a protégé of Barbara Bartholic. I worked closely with Barbara for many years and was able to gain a better understanding of my own alien abduction experiences through my close relationship with Barbara. In so doing I was able to help other abductees who sought me out in order to gain a better understanding of their own experiences. I am but one of countless people who have greatly benefited from Barbara's sage advice and counsel. The first and foremost of Barbara's protégés was the late great Dr. Karla "Kandy" Turner. Barbara Bartholic and Kandy Turner formed the greatest partnership in UFO Research history. Barbara worked behind the scenes and Kandy brought the findings of Barbara to the attention of the UFO Research Community. Kandy became an outstanding alien abduction researcher in her own right. Kandy and her family were alien abductees who had obtained help from Barbara.

Bartley goes own to say that Barbara realized that "energetic harvesting" was a principal component of the alien abduction syndrome and that she knew that negative aliens (like the Reptilians) "manipulated the energy centres and emotions of alien abductees in order to nourish and empower themselves at the expense of the abductees." This concept is a massively important one in Satanism and conspiracy research since this exact phenomenon is being played out on a planetary-wide scale. I briefly touched on this earlier when I mentioned loosh. The Satanists act as perpetrators to feed off the blood and energy of innocent victims, although it would appear that the Satanists themselves are also a victim of a darker force (the Reptilians, or whatever force is controlling them) which bewitches, hypnotizes and controls them, and thus are not ultimately at the top of the pyramid. To say more about this here is beyond the scope of this book, however those interested can read more in my book *Break Your Chains: Exposing the Worldwide Conspiracy and Presenting the Way Out*[51] and research the concepts of the Archons, Djinn and Wetiko (different words, same force);

– James Bartley, who as mentioned above is a protégé of Barbara. James has been researching alien abductions and the military connection to UFOs and aliens for 25 years.

---

[51] https://www.amazon.com/Break-Your-Chains-Conspiracy-Presenting/dp/B0CCCX8NTZ

According to his website[52], James spent a lot of time "conducting field investigations in the High Desert of Southern California, Arizona and Nevada. He specializes in research and investigations into Reptilian Aliens and Military Abductions." James has many of his own personal encounters with Reptilians over the years and deeply understands the topic; and

– the late Dr. Karla Turner, who again as mentioned above is a protégé of Barbara. Karla wrote books such as *Taken: Inside the Alien-Human Abduction Agenda*[53] and *Into The Fringe: A True Story of Alien Abduction*[54] where she documented the very real phenomenon of reptilian abduction.

There are plenty of other sources out there for those interested. Some of those with personal experiences of the Reptilians are covered in my book *40 Incredible Real Life Alien Abductee and Contactee Experiences –*

---

[52] https://www.thecosmicswitchboard.com/about-james/

[53] https://www.amazon.com/Taken-Inside-Alien-Human-Abduction-Agenda/dp/1490459081/

[54] https://www.amazon.com/Into-Fringe-Story-Alien-Abduction/dp/1495902757/

Controversial Truths Revealed Series Book 2[55].

[55] https://www.amazon.com/Incredible-Alien-Abductee-Contactee-Experiences-ebook/dp/B0BG6G9D4P/

Chapter 17 – Other Testimonies

There are many other non-victim/non-survivor sources of information about Satanism, too many for this book. The topic of Satanism occasionally reaches the ears of the general public via the Mainstream Media, such as in this video[56] of an old Oprah show where people reported ritual human sacrifice.

Another way the information gets out is via therapists, since due to the nature of their profession, they are hearing people's inner feelings and deeper secrets. They also provide a safe space for hidden memories to surface, memories which are subliminal (beyond the threshold of the conscious mind). A fascinating example is Canadian psychotherapist Sandra Fecht, who had no idea about SRA until her clients started regressing, then recalling the sexual abuse they suffered at rituals with child sacrifice and lizard people (Reptilians). At first she thought the whole thing was imagined, however she kept hearing the same theme over and over from different clients. She became determined to investigate it further, but was threatened to back off. Then, her office was spray painted with Satanic symbols. Eventually, she came to realize how powerful the underground Satanic-Masonic

---

[56] https://www.youtube.com/watch?v=5s3oBz40msM

network is with its control of politics, police, intelligence, media and more. An interview where she revealed all this is still available on the Wayback Machine (Internet Archive) here[57].

---

[57] https://web.archive.org/web/20150825073510/https://www.youtube.com/watch?v=cw_Wr7trX24

Chapter 18 – Satanic Sites

The curious reader may at this point be wondering where Satanic ritual is practiced. The general answer is inside elite bloodline mansions (such as those belonging to the Rothschilds and Rockefellers), at certain European castles, at certain sacred sites and even within certain churches or centers of government. Recall that Fiona Barnett's testimony includes references to Satanic rituals, orgies and sacrifice being performed at Australia's Parliament House, some survivors mention the British Parliament and many survivors talk about the White House. Stanley Kubrick's iconic film (and his last before he died of a mysterious heart attack), Eyes Wide Shut, contains an unforgettable and highly significant scene of Satanic ritual and orgy inside an elite mansion. Kubrick actually found a Rothschild mansion in the UK and managed to shoot the scene there.

However, there is a place that stands out among survivor testimony. It lies deep in the forest of Belgium, close to the border with France. It is the Chateau des Amerois or "Mothers of Darkness" Castle (see right), said to be home to Satanic Illuminati rituals, orgies, blackmail parties and human sacrifice. The castle is shrouded in mystery, and reportedly has an ornate room with a domed ceiling with 1000 lights in it. Ex-President and Satanist George H. W. Bush often mentioned "1000 points of light" in his speeches, obliquely referring to this.

According to Jessie Czebotar, the Mothers of Darkness Castle is the place where high level Illuminati witches are trained castle using MK Ultra techniques.

Chateau des Amerois

The Chateau des Amerois was formerly owned by the Saxe-Gotha-Coburg family (one of the infamous British Royal Family bloodlines, now known as the Windsors, who changed their name in 1917 for public relations reason since Britain was then at war with Germany). The Windsors, of course, are one of the major hybrid Reptilian-human bloodlines as explained earlier. The castle was later sold to the Solvay Group before World War I. The Solvay Group is involved with selling sodium fluoride[58] to municipalities for water fluoridation – itself another massive scam that puts toxic fluoride into people's bodies, thus lowering their IQ and leading to a host of other problems, for little to no benefit[59].

This website[60] says the following:

"In their 2001 book dedicated to the Dutroux affair, "Dossier pédophilie. Le scandale de l'affaire Dutroux" (Paedophilia File: The Scandal of the Dutroux Affair) p. 259, Jean Nicolas and Frédéric Lavachery mention the Amerois castle as a place where satanic ritual parties and child sacrifices took place. A report of the Dutroux affair refers to the letter of a retired Gendarme (police man) talking about this castle. The book has reports from a Dutch priest that it was a place where satanic soirées took place with child sacrifices. An American solider from NATO, who took part to one of these parties and felt disgusted, supposedly gave this information to the Dutch."

---

58 https://www.solvay.com/sites/g/files/srpend221/files/2021-01/PSS-Sodium-Fluoride.pdf

59 https://fluoridealert.org/wp-content/uploads/FAN-Neurotoxicity-flyer-5-23-23-B-Final.pdf

60 https://mymkultra.wordpress.com/2022/07/30/mother-of-darkness-castle/

Glamis Castle

Glamis Castle (pronounced 'Glarmz', see right) has been the home of the Lyons family since the 14th century, though the present building dates largely from the 17th century. The Lyons family is another European 'royal' bloodline. Glamis was the childhood home of the now deceased Queen Elizabeth and Queen Mother. Glamis Castle is situated beside the village of Glamis in Angus, Scotland.

In addition to Chateau Amerois and Glamis Castle, Arizona Wilder claims that Satanic

ritual is conducted at Balmoral Castle (see left), at Westminster Abbey (a famous church in England in the center of London) and at the sacred site Stonehenge. This goes along with what other survivors have said regarding the use of sacred churches, temples and sites for Satanic use when no one is looking (e.g. Chantal Frei and at La Sagrada Familia).

Arizona also states that Marquis de Libeaux (who she believes is Pindar, top of the Satanic hierarchy) has a castle in France in the Alsace-Lorraine region. She claims that this castle hides an entrance to an underground system of caves with formations of rocks that naturally glow green. She claims that the Satanist Reptilians, who worship menstrual blood, store it in these rock formations. This transforms the green glow and makes it darker; they call it "black blood" and used it in certain rituals. Arizona also claims reptilian pets, and nests of eggs, are kept down in these caves to incubate.

Chapter 19 – Healing from Satanic Ritual Abuse

A common theme among SRA survivors is that they have turned to a higher power – whether through Christianity, another organized religion or spirituality – to help them become whole. Many have also put a painstaking number of hours into therapy, working with a trusted therapist or therapists, to gradually uncover all the memories deep beneath the surface, bringing them to light so that they may be healed.

Kathy Collins (chapter 7) is noteworthy in this area. Through determination and lots of self-work, Kathy was able to heal the horrific traumas she underwent. In the aforementioned interview with Bill Ryan, she shares what she has learned and experienced about healing trauma:

– Healing trauma is not about getting to a particular place (it's not goal-oriented and linear). It's best not to be rushed, but rather about mastering the moment, mastering your reaction, making the pain your friend – after all, the pain is just a messenger, so try to understand what it is trying to tell you. Denying it only makes it continue;

– It is very helpful to learn techniques to deal with suppressed memories as they arise;

– A shift happens when you take responsibility for your own actions. This includes not playing the victim. Kathy didn't realize she was thinking, identifying and acting like a victim, and that therefore this recreated trauma. As humans, we recreate the familiar. We need serotonin to live, and trauma victims have learnt to create serotonin through trauma and drama. Kathy learnt how to get serotonin from sunsets;

– Transformation occurs when you move into forgiveness, i.e. look back at the past without any judgement attached to it. Then, you can actually see it as a gift. Like the comic stories of superheroes who need a challenge/bad guy to know how strong and courageous they were, we can use trauma to know how powerful we are. From the right perspective, it becomes a gift because it forced us to grow;

– If you are a SRA victim, you are not alone; there are millions of people who have gone through these things. You may need a village to help you fully heal;

– Allow the body to teach the mind (see the research of Peter Levine). The body may feel something (fear, pain) before the mind knows it;

– Lastly, Kathy discovered that for healing, the following things are essential:

1. A sense of humor: Norman Cousins healed himself of cancer through humor and laughing. Being able to laugh at things makes you lighter and freer;

2. Mindfulness: mindfully choose to be around people who are uplifting. Be mindful of your thoughts and emotions. Be mindful of that upon which you dwell, because what you focus on you create, and the chronic pain can be hard not to focus on. Be aware that there is a self-destruct/suicide program installed in many mind control victims;

3. Dedication: you need a strong and constant commitment to your own healing in order to overcome cycles of overwhelm and depression; and

4. Self-love: you must love all the parts of yourself, no matter how dark they seem, to become a fully integrated human being.

In many ways, the NWO controllers are more focused on fantasy than reality, because they understand the power of imagination in creating what is to come. They hijack the mass public's imagination (and thus ability to create) via control of the mass media and entertainment industries, through which they program the masses to create a reality and a world that best suits the NWO controllers, not which best suits the general public and average person. Thus, healing from SRA necessarily involves deprogramming from mind control.

For SRA victims, the individual journey of traumatization, realization and transformation are a microcosm of the collective human journey.

If you are a recovering ritual abuse or mind control survivor, please remember: it is possible to reclaim your humanity even if you have been through horrible trauma. We can make our present and future into one of fulfillment, contentedness and happiness, as long as we choose to frame what happened in the past in an empowering way (a challenge or gift that helped us grow and gave us wisdom) rather than a disempowering way (something that scarred us forever and made us into a permanent victim). There are survivor organizations all around the world whose sole mission is to assist with ritual abuse and mind control recovery.

Chapter 20 – Conclusion

The point of this book is to give the reader an introductory glimpse into the very real world of Satanism. This book could have included so many more voices. There are a plethora of survivors around the world. Websites such as this one (50 Voices of Ritual Abuse[61]) contain video testimony of those who've been through it. Many of the survivors in this book have written their own books about their experiences.

The information I have presented so far has been voluminous, so I will finish by summarizing it all. Here is an organized overview of what we know about the international Satanic network:

– While there many be many forms of Satanism practiced, and many Satanic churches, groups and organizations in the world, an overarching international Satanic network exists. This network is highly organized and efficiently run with a strict hierarchy, consisting of branches or divisions in different countries and in a way similar to a multinational corporation;

– Satanism is an inversion of the natural state of the world. It inverts language, mathematics, symbols, art and many other things to promote the diametric opposite of

61 https://www.50voices.org/en/start-en/

what was originally intended. The word 'Satan' means 'opposer.' The word 'evil' is 'live' spelt backwards. This truth is reflected in George Orwell's 1984 dystopic slogan "War Is Peace. Freedom Is Slavery. Ignorance Is Strength" as it is a complete inversion of the truth;

– SRA tends to run in families. They recruit children at a very young age to be programmed using sophisticated mind control techniques. It is often perpetuated within a family over generations. Sometimes, the head of the cult teaches (or programs) the children and grandchildren to treat those weaker than them or dependent upon them cruelly. In some cases, SRA victims are selected before birth for certain roles, and it is common that parents are encouraged to sell their children into the cult to make money off them. This is why Satanism is inseparable from slavery, pedophilia and sex trafficking;

– As young children, often SRA victims are abused by teenagers and adults. This is a feature of the system: those on top abuse those below, all the way throughout the Satanic hierarchy;

– The programming is often repeated over and over, using the same themes: Monarch butterflies, Wizard of Oz symbolism ('over the rainbow') and dolphins. Sometimes, children are deliberately created to be inducted into the Satanic cult and given the same name (e.g. little girl Bush Babies are named 'Kelly);'

– The victims are abused and tortured in any different ways in order to break them down and make them susceptible to mind control programming. These techniques were perfected by the CIA in its MK Ultra projects which spanned decades. The victims are almost always selected as children, since the abuse leads them to disassociate, thus creating different personalities or alters within their mind, with each alter unaware of the others. This leads to the development of MPD or DID. The most common ways these mind controlled victims were used were as spies, couriers, sex slaves and assassins;

– The reason why the Satanists have gotten away with so much of this is because they control key positions of power in society, including the media (which can choose not to report on Satanism) and the police/judiciary (which can shut down investigations and dismiss lawsuits that get too close to the truth). Additionally, the Satanists set up organizations like 'false memory foundations' to convince the public and psychologists that people recalling their very real experiences in the Satanic cult are crazy and delusional;

– The Satanic realm overlaps with other realms, including those involving 'plain' or non-Satanic torture, rape, sexual abuse, mind control, human sacrifice, ritual killing, cannibalism and others. Not everyone who engages in these activities is necessarily Satanic, however true Satanists will engage in these activities as part of their devotion to Satanism;

- The Satanic NWO manipulators follow the law of black magician Aleister Crowley - "Do What Thou Wilt" - as their highest principle. They live like their actions have no consequences. They use their money and power in the real world to cover up their crimes;

- Satanism is inextricably connected with the use of black magic, i.e. the use of higher human powers like imagination, creation and manifestation in a way that harms others. There are at least two main purposes of the various elements of Satanism - ritual, costume, abuse, torture, mind control, sex, sacrifice, murder and cannibalism. The first is to induce the participants into high and altered states of consciousness where something akin to demonic possession happens, where they enter into a frequency match with entities in another dimension, and direct 2-way communication can occur. These otherworldly or interdimensional entities can then directly convey commands or program those who open themselves up to these entities. The second is for the Reptilians, and their hybrid half-reptilian, half-human bloodlines, to produce enough terror in their victims so as to get them to secrete certain hormones into their blood (e.g. adrenochrome), which the Reptilians and hybrids can then consume as life force energy, to help them sustain their human form and existence in this realm;

– Satanism involves the use of 'breeders' or human females to produce babies who are then either intentionally aborted to be killed in Satanic ritual, or who are inducted into the Satanic cult from birth to be groomed for future roles within the network;

– Many survivors who escaped the Satanic cult attest to the fact that there is a human hunting game, where children are let loose then literally hunted to death like animals; and

– Satanism is run by entities that are cut off from their own life-force energy, and thus need to exploit other creatures for their energy. They have worked out how to set up a situation where they manipulate people into low vibrational states (despair, terror, fear) in order to feed off that emotional energy.

If you have made it this far to the very end, well done. There is no doubt that Satanism plumbs the very depths of evil. It is truly sickening and horrific. It is hard to imagine anything worse. However, denial, though more comfortable, is not an adequate answer to this evil. We must face the ugly truth of Satanism and the international Satanic network if we want to stop it and transform it. After all, these practicing Satanists are composed of the most rich and powerful people in the world. For them, this isn't just some side hobby; it directly affects who they are. The Satanic influence on their mindset translates into governmental policy. Indeed, it is no exaggeration to say that it dictates how the world is run, both in mission and manner. The NWO is underpinned by Satanism. It is no exaggeration to say that Satanism is playing a key role in bringing about a tyrannical world dictatorship. The Satanic hierarchy comes before other governmental or business hierarchies visible to the public. Satanism is the guiding force for the dysfunction in the world today on a grand scale.

My hope is that, armed with this knowledge, people can realize the true forces directing world affairs and our (mis)leaders, continue exposing Satanism, overcome its negative influence, step into their power and reclaim their minds – to use their imagination and manifestation from a place of sovereignty to create a world of peace, abundance and freedom.

Printed in Great Britain
by Amazon

41407899R00066